FEEDBACK MASTERY

Playbook for Effective Team Communication

Dr Nils Koenig

FEEDBACK MASTERY

Playbook for Effective Team Communication

Copyright © 2024 Dr Nils Koenig

All rights reserved. This publication, or any part thereof, may not be reproduced in any form or by any means, including electronic, photographic, or mechanical, or by any sound recording system, or by any device for storage and retrieval of information, without the written permission of the copyright owner.

CONTENTS

INTRODUCTION: The Power of Feedback in a Fast-Changing World — 1

CHAPTER 1: Introduction to Feedback — 7

CHAPTER 2: How to Give Feedback Effectively — 15

CHAPTER 3: Alternative and Advanced Feedback Techniques — 23

CHAPTER 4: How to Receive Feedback Effectively — 35

CHAPTER 5: Evaluating Feedback Effectiveness — 43

CHAPTER 6: Feedback Across Cultures — 51

CHAPTER 7: Strengthen Your Team's Feedback Muscle with Feedback Cards and Exercises — 59

CHAPTER 8: Additional Exercises to Practice Feedback Giving and Receiving — 71

CONCLUSION: Mastering Feedback for Team Development and Continuous Improvement — 89

INTRODUCTION
The Power of Feedback in a Fast-Changing World

THE POWER OF FEEDBACK IN A FAST-CHANGING WORLD

In today's fast-paced, ever-evolving work environment, the ability to give and receive feedback is more critical than ever. Rapid technological advancements, shifting market demands, and evolving workplace dynamics require organizations to be agile, innovative, and resilient. At the heart of these capabilities lies effective feedback.

Feedback is not just a tool for correction; it is a catalyst for growth, learning, and continuous improvement. In a world where change is the only constant, feedback helps individuals and teams navigate complexities, adapt to new challenges, and drive performance to new heights. This playbook is designed to equip you with the skills and practices necessary to master the art of feedback, ensuring that it becomes an integral part of your organizational culture.

The Increased Need for Feedback

As organizations face unprecedented change, the need for timely, constructive feedback has intensified. Employees must adapt to new technologies, workflows, and expectations quickly. Line managers, in turn, must guide their teams through these transitions, ensuring that everyone remains aligned with the organization's goals and values. Feedback serves as a vital mechanism to facilitate this alignment and promote a culture of continuous learning and improvement.

Benefits of an Improved Feedback Culture

Actively working on and improving how your team uses feedback enhances your overall team culture and atmosphere, but also generates very direct benefits for the team's management and every member:

For Line Managers	For Team Members
1. **Enhanced Performance Management:** Regular feedback helps line managers identify areas of improvement and recognize achievements, leading to more effective performance management.	1. **Personal and Professional Growth:** Feedback provides employees with insights into their strengths and areas for development, guiding their personal and professional growth.
2. **Stronger Team Dynamics:** Constructive feedback fosters open communication and trust, enhancing team cohesion and collaboration.	2. **Increased Engagement and Motivation:** When employees feel their contributions are recognized and valued, their engagement and motivation levels rise.
3. **Proactive Problem Solving:** Timely feedback allows managers to address issues before they escalate, promoting a proactive approach to problem-solving.	3. **Improved Job Satisfaction:** A culture of feedback fosters a supportive work environment where employees feel heard and appreciated, leading to higher job satisfaction.

4. **Leadership Development:** Providing and receiving feedback helps managers refine their leadership skills, becoming more empathetic, communicative, and effective leaders.

4. **Skill Enhancement:** Constructive feedback helps employees refine their skills and improve their performance, contributing to their overall career development.

Feedback: An Essential Skill for Organizational Development

Feedback is not a one-time event but an ongoing process that fuels organizational development. It helps create a culture where continuous improvement is embraced, innovation is encouraged, and employees are empowered to reach their full potential. To build and expand this "feedback muscle," it must be exercised regularly and applied consistently across all levels of the organization.

This playbook is designed to provide you with the tools, techniques, and exercises needed to develop a robust feedback culture. By integrating these practices into your daily interactions, you will not only enhance individual and team performance but also drive your organization toward greater agility, innovation, and success.

Welcome to the journey of mastering feedback – a journey that will transform the way you communicate, collaborate, and grow in today's fast-changing world. Let's build and strengthen our feedback muscles together, ensuring that our organizations thrive in the face of continuous change.

CHAPTER 1
Introduction to Feedback

What is Feedback?

Feedback is a critical communication tool that helps individuals understand how their actions and behaviors are perceived by others. It involves providing constructive insights, observations, and suggestions aimed at improving performance, enhancing skills, and fostering personal and professional growth. Effective feedback is:

- **Descriptive:** Focuses on specific behaviors and observations rather than personal attributes.
- **Actionable:** Provides clear, practical advice that can be implemented for improvement.
- **Supportive:** Encourages positive change and development.

Why Feedback Matters

Feedback plays a vital role in various aspects of personal and organizational development:

1. **Improves Team Performance and Productivity:** Feedback helps align individual efforts with team and organizational goals. By addressing issues and reinforcing positive behaviors, feedback ensures that the team operates efficiently and effectively, contributing to overall productivity.

2. **Builds Trust and Strengthens Relationships:** Regular, constructive feedback fosters open communication and transparency. When team members feel that their contributions are recognized and valued, trust is built, leading to stronger, more collaborative relationships.
3. **Facilitates Continuous Improvement and Learning:** Feedback encourages a culture of continuous improvement. It motivates individuals to strive for excellence and fosters an environment where learning and development are prioritized.
4. **Enhances Personal Growth:** Feedback provides individuals with insights into their strengths and areas for improvement. It helps them understand how their actions impact others and offers guidance on how to enhance their skills and behaviors.

Feedback as a Precondition for Building an Effective and Resilient Team

To build an effective and resilient team, feedback must be integrated into the fabric of the team's culture. Here's how feedback contributes to this goal:

1. **Promotes Accountability and Responsibility:** Regular feedback ensures that team members are aware of their responsibilities and the

impact of their actions. It promotes a sense of accountability, where individuals take ownership of their performance and work towards collective success.

2. **Aligns Individual and Team Goals:** Feedback helps align individual performance with team and organizational objectives. It ensures that everyone is working towards the same goals, promoting coherence and unity within the team.
3. **Encourages Adaptability and Innovation:** In a rapidly changing environment, teams must be adaptable and innovative. Feedback provides the necessary insights for individuals to adjust their behaviors and approaches, fostering a culture that embraces change and seeks creative solutions.
4. **Enhances Communication and Collaboration:** Effective feedback improves communication within the team. By openly discussing strengths and areas for improvement, team members can collaborate more effectively, leveraging each other's skills and knowledge to achieve common goals.
5. **Builds Resilience and Coping Mechanisms:** Feedback helps individuals and teams navigate challenges and setbacks.

Constructive feedback provides the guidance needed to overcome obstacles and develop resilience. It enables team members to learn from their experiences and emerge stronger.

6. **Fosters a Positive Work Environment:** When feedback is given and received positively, it creates a supportive and motivating work environment. Team members feel valued and understood, which boosts morale and job satisfaction, leading to higher retention and engagement rates.

Dispelling Myths and Misconceptions About Feedback

Feedback is an essential tool for personal and professional growth, yet many myths and misconceptions persist about how it should be delivered. These outdated practices can hinder effective communication and even damage relationships within a team. In fact, it is one of the primary motivations for writing this playbook to address these misconceptions and provide a more effective approach to giving and receiving feedback. Let us look at a few common misconceptions about feedback:

The Feedback Sandwich: The "feedback sandwich" method, where negative feedback is sandwiched between two pieces of positive feedback, is a widely taught technique. The idea is to cushion the blow of criticism with praise. While it aims to soften the impact of negative feedback, this method can lead to distrust. Recipients may begin to associate positive comments with impending criticism, undermining genuine praise and leading to anxiety and skepticism.

Feedback Should Always Be Positive: To avoid hurt feelings, some believe that feedback should focus solely on positive aspects. But constructive criticism, when delivered appropriately, is essential for growth and improvement. Avoiding necessary corrective feedback can prevent team members from learning and developing their skills.

Feedback is Only for Poor Performers: Others believe that feedback is primarily for those who are underperforming and need correction. Everyone, including high performers, will benefit from constructive and tailored feedback. It can reinforce positive behaviors, encourage continuous improvement, and maintain high performance levels.

Immediate Feedback is Always Best: Many people will tell you that feedback should be given immediately after the observed behavior to be effective. Now, while timely feedback is important, it should also be considerate of the recipient's state of mind and context. Immediate feedback can sometimes catch someone off guard or be delivered without adequate thought, reducing its effectiveness.

Feedback is One-Way Communication: The stereotypical view is that feedback is something a manager gives to a subordinate. In fact, effective feedback is a two-way dialogue. Encouraging feedback from all directions—peer-to-peer, upward, and self-assessment—creates a more dynamic and supportive environment.

The persistence of outdated feedback practices can have several detrimental effects on team dynamics and overall performance. One significant issue is the **erosion of trust**, particularly with methods like the feedback sandwich. Over time, team members may become suspicious of positive comments, anticipating that negative feedback will follow, which undermines genuine praise and fosters a sense of distrust. Additionally, ineffective feedback techniques can lead to **misunderstandings**, reducing the likelihood that feedback will be acted upon constructively. This can diminish the feedback's overall effectiveness and prevent meaningful improvements. Furthermore, inadequate or poorly delivered feedback can **hurt team morale**, making individuals feel undervalued or unfairly criticized, which can lead to disengagement and decreased motivation. The absence of honest and constructive feedback can also cause **stagnation**, as individuals and teams struggle to identify areas for improvement and innovation, hindering their growth and development. Finally, mishandled feedback can create **conflict and resentment among team members**, damaging cohesion and productivity. These negative outcomes highlight the importance of adopting effective feedback practices to maintain a healthy and productive team environment.

> *To counter these myths and their adverse effects, this playbook offers a comprehensive guide to mastering feedback. By understanding and implementing effective feedback practices, you can foster a culture of continuous improvement, trust, and open communication within your team. This playbook is designed to help you move away from ineffective methods and towards a more dynamic and supportive approach to feedback. It will guide you through the best practices for giving and receiving feedback, ensuring that your team can leverage this powerful tool to achieve success.*

CHAPTER 2
How to Give Feedback Effectively

Key Principles of Giving Feedback

Giving effective feedback is a skill that requires thoughtfulness and precision. Here are the key principles to keep in mind:

1. Descriptive, Not Evaluative
Focus on personal observations without making judgments.
Example: *"I noticed you interrupted John several times during the meeting,"* instead of *"You were rude to John."*

2. Clear and Precise
Ensure your feedback is easy to understand and well-articulated.
Example: *"Your report was thorough and well-organized, but it would be more effective with a summary at the beginning."*

3. Factually Correct
Base your feedback on verifiable observations.
Example: *"Your email lacked the project details we discussed,"* instead of *"You never provide enough information."*

4. Free of Moral Judgment
Avoid moral implications to reduce defensive reactions.

Example: *"The project deadline was missed,"* instead of *"You were irresponsible with the deadline."*

5. Specific, Not General
Detail exact behaviors rather than vague character critiques.
Example: *"You were 15 minutes late to the client meeting on Tuesday,"* instead of *"You are always late."*

6. Observation-Based, Not Assumptive
Rely on what is directly seen, avoiding guesses or interpretations.
Example: *"You left the office early three times last week,"* instead of *"You don't care about your work."*

7. Focused on Changeable Behaviors
Concentrate on aspects that the individual can influence or adjust.
Example: *"Please ensure you proofread your emails before sending,"* instead of *"Your emails are always full of errors."*

8. Solicited, Not Imposed
Feedback is most effective when requested by the recipient.
Example: *"Can I offer some feedback on your presentation?"* instead of *"Here's what you did wrong in your presentation."*

9. Considerate of the Recipient's Needs
Be mindful of how the feedback will impact the recipient, aiming to be helpful rather than harmful.
Example: *"I know you've been under a lot of pressure, but I wanted to discuss how we can improve our communication."*

10. Timely
Provide feedback soon after the relevant behavior to ensure relevance and clarity, while considering the recipient's emotional state.
Example: *"Let's discuss the project results from last week,"* instead of *"Remember that project from six months ago?"*

The WWW Model for Giving Feedback

A structured approach to giving feedback ensures clarity and effectiveness. The WWW model is a simple and practical framework:

1. What I Observed:
Begin by describing specifically what you observed, sticking to facts and clear examples.
Example: *"During our team meeting yesterday, I noticed that you provided a lot of valuable insights on the project."*

2. Why It Matters:
Explain the impact of the observed behavior. Discuss how it affects you, the team, or the project.
Example: *"Your insights helped clarify our strategy, which will improve our chances of meeting the project deadline."*

3. What I Wish:
Conclude by expressing a constructive wish or suggestion for future behavior.
Example: *"I wish you would share your ideas more often in meetings, as they are very helpful to the team's progress."*

Practical Tips for Giving Feedback

1. Prepare in Advance:
Think through what you want to say and how you will say it. Preparation helps you provide clear and concise feedback.

2. Choose the Right Setting:
Provide feedback in a private and comfortable setting to avoid embarrassment and encourage open dialogue.

3. Use "I" Statements:
Frame your feedback from your perspective to avoid sounding accusatory.

Example: *"I feel concerned when deadlines are missed because it impacts the whole team."*

4. Be Positive and Constructive:
Balance negative feedback with positive comments. Highlight what was done well and suggest improvements.

Example: *"Your report was detailed and well-researched. It would be even better with a clearer summary at the start."*

5. Be Patient and Open:
Allow the recipient time to process the feedback and respond. Be open to their perspective and any questions they may have.

Examples of Effective Feedback
Let's look at a few examples how feedback could be given, depending on the topic and scenario:

1. Performance Feedback:
Scenario: A team member consistently meets their sales targets.
Feedback: *"I'm impressed with how consistently you meet your sales targets. Your approach to client relationships is outstanding. I'd love to see you share your strategies with the team to help us all improve."*

2. Behavioral Feedback:

Scenario: A team member frequently interrupts others during meetings.

Feedback: *"During meetings, I've noticed that you often interrupt others while they're speaking. This can disrupt the flow of discussion and cause frustration. I'd appreciate it if you could wait until others have finished speaking before sharing your thoughts."*

3. Developmental Feedback:

Scenario: A team member shows potential but lacks confidence in presentations.

Feedback: *"You have a lot of valuable insights, but I've noticed you seem hesitant when presenting. With a bit more practice and preparation, I believe you could become a very effective presenter. How about we arrange some practice sessions?"*

> By adhering to these principles and using the WWW model, you can provide feedback that is clear, constructive, and impactful. This will help foster a positive and productive team environment where continuous improvement is embraced.

CHAPTER 3
Alternative and Advanced Feedback Techniques

ALTERNATIVE AND ADVANCED FEEDBACK TECHNIQUES

Chapter 2 covered some basic aspects of feedback and gave a lot of practical advice on how to best give feedback. This chapter provides some alternative models to help you formulate the feedback. These may be especially helpful when the feedback is complex or as a way to reframe and rephrase when the feedback has not been properly understood by the recipient.

SBI Model: Situation-Behavior-Impact

The Situation-Behavior-Impact (SBI) model is a structured approach to providing feedback that helps ensure clarity and effectiveness. This model focuses on describing specific situations, the observed behaviors within those situations, and the impact of those behaviors. By sticking to concrete observations and their direct consequences, the SBI model helps in delivering feedback that is clear, objective, and actionable. It uses three steps:

S	B	I
The **Situation** – Time and place where the act ion happened	The **Behavior** – The actions we're giving feedback for.	The **Impact** – The ways in which the behavior impacts us.
Describe the specific situation where the behavior was observed. This	Detail the behavior you observed without making judgments or assumptions. Focus	Explain the impact of the behavior on you, the team, or the project. This shows why the

FEEDBACK MASTERY

sets the context and helps the recipient understand when and where the behavior occurred.	on what was seen or heard.	behavior matters and helps the recipient understand its consequences.
Example: *"During our team meeting on Monday..."*	Example: *"...you interrupted John several times while he was presenting his ideas..."*	Example: *"...which caused confusion and frustration among the team, disrupting the flow of the meeting."*

Here are a few more practical examples of SBI Feedback, illustrating how the model can be used to deliver clear, objective, and impactful feedback that helps recipients understand specific behaviors and their consequences, leading to constructive conversations and improvements.

Situation	"In our team meeting last Thursday..."	"In your email response to the customer last Tuesday..."	"During our conference call with the partner company last Thursday..."
Behavior	"...you provided a detailed overview of the project timeline and	"...you addressed all their concerns promptly and offered a	"...you frequently checked your phone and seemed distracted."

25

	addressed all the critical milestones clearly."	clear solution to their issue."	
Impact	"...which helped the team understand the project better and ensured everyone was aligned on the next steps."	"...which resulted in positive feedback from the customer and enhanced our reputation for excellent customer service."	"...which gave the impression that you were not fully engaged in the discussion, potentially undermining our professionalism and commitment."

Feedforward Technique

The Feedforward technique shifts the focus from past behaviors to future actions. Instead of dwelling on what went wrong, it emphasizes what can be done differently moving forward. This approach is particularly useful in motivating and guiding team members towards positive changes without triggering defensiveness.

← Feedback	Feedforward →
<ul><li>Focuses on the past</li><li>Criticizes previous work</li><li>Points out problems</li><li>Limited and static</li></ul>	<ul><li>Focuses on the future</li><li>Suggests what to do next time</li><li>Focuses in the task, not the person</li></ul>

• Can be an "information dump" • Doesn't always offer a plan of action • Can lead to people feeling judged and becoming defensive	• Expands possibilities • Is particular • Helps an employee to create a specific plan for improvement • Can help motivate people

To use Feedforward effectively, look at the following three steps:

1. Identify the Goal:
Start by discussing the goal or the desired outcome the team member should aim for.
Example: *"Our goal is to enhance client satisfaction in our upcoming projects."*

2. Suggest Future Actions:
Provide specific suggestions or actions that the team member can take to achieve the goal. Focus on positive and constructive advice.
Example: *"In future client meetings, try to summarize the key points at the end to ensure the client feels heard and understood."*

3. Encourage Reflection and Agreement: Encourage the team member to reflect on the suggestions and agree on the next steps. This ensures buy-in and commitment to the new approach.

Example: *"How do you feel about this approach? Do you think summarizing key points will help in our next meeting?"*

Here are some practical examples to illustrate the Feedforward technique:

Goal	Future action
"We want to improve our team's collaboration during projects."	*"In our next project, let's start each meeting with a quick round of updates from each member. This will help everyone stay informed and engaged."*
"Enhance customer service response times."	*"Moving forward, let's establish a protocol where all customer inquiries are acknowledged within one hour, even if a full resolution takes longer. This will help manage customer expectations and improve satisfaction."*
"Increase employee engagement in meetings."	*"For our upcoming meetings, let's encourage everyone to prepare one idea or question in advance. This will ensure active participation and make our discussions more dynamic and productive."*
"Enhance personal time management skills."	*"Going forward, try using a time management tool like Trello or Asana to prioritize and track your tasks. Setting daily goals and reviewing your progress at the end of each day can help improve your time management skills."*

"Boost the quality of project deliverables."	"In future projects, let's implement a peer review system where each deliverable is reviewed by a colleague before submission. This will help catch errors early and improve the overall quality of our work."

Handling Defensive Reactions

When providing feedback, it's not uncommon to encounter defensive reactions. These reactions can stem from a variety of reasons, including fear of criticism, lack of self-awareness, or previous negative experiences with feedback. Managing these reactions effectively is crucial for maintaining a productive dialogue and ensuring the feedback is received constructively. Here are some tips and strategies for managing defensive reactions:

1. Stay Calm and Patient:
Maintain a calm and composed demeanor. This helps de-escalate the situation and shows that you are open to dialogue.
Strategy: Take deep breaths and speak in a steady, non-confrontational tone.

2. Use Empathy and Understanding:
Show empathy by acknowledging the recipient's feelings and perspectives. This helps build trust and openness.

Strategy: *"I understand that this feedback might be hard to hear. I'm here to support you and work through this together."*

3. Focus on the Behavior, Not the Person:
Emphasize that the feedback is about specific behaviors and not a judgment of the person's character or abilities.
Strategy: *"I noticed that the report was submitted late. I'm not questioning your dedication, but I want to understand what caused the delay."*

4. Ask Open-Ended Questions:
Encourage the recipient to share their perspective and thoughts. This can help uncover underlying issues and promote a collaborative solution.
Strategy: *"Can you tell me more about what challenges you faced with this project?"*

5. Offer Support and Resources:
Show that you are willing to provide help and resources to address the issues raised in the feedback.
Strategy: *"Would additional training or resources help you manage your time better for future projects?"*

6. Follow Up:
Arrange a follow-up meeting to discuss progress and provide ongoing support. This demonstrates your commitment to their development and reinforces the importance of the feedback.

Strategy: *"Let's meet again in two weeks to see how things are going and discuss any further support you might need."*

Here are some practical examples of handling defensive reactions by staying calm, showing empathy, focusing on specific behaviors, and offering constructive solutions, thereby fostering a positive and productive feedback environment.

Feedback	Defensive Reaction	Response
"I've noticed that you've missed several deadlines recently, which has affected the project timeline."	*"I've been overwhelmed with work, and it's not fair to blame me for this."*	*"I understand that you're feeling overwhelmed. Let's discuss what we can do to manage your workload better and ensure we meet our deadlines."*
"I've noticed that your project reports often contain several errors, which impacts our team's efficiency."	*"It's not fair to single me out. Everyone makes mistakes in their reports."*	*"I understand that errors can happen to anyone. Let's work together to find a way to minimize these mistakes. Would you find it helpful to have a second pair of eyes review your reports before submission?"*

ALTERNATIVE AND ADVANCED FEEDBACK TECHNIQUES

"You've been arriving late to our team meetings, which affects our ability to start on time."	"Traffic is always bad in the morning. I can't control that."	"I understand that traffic can be unpredictable. Let's discuss some possible solutions, like leaving a bit earlier or exploring alternative routes, to help ensure you can arrive on time."
"During client calls, you often speak over others, which can come across as unprofessional."	"I only do that because I want to make sure my point is heard. It's important."	"I appreciate your enthusiasm and the points you bring up are valuable. Let's work on finding the right moments to interject, so we can maintain a respectful and professional tone during calls."
"I've noticed that your tone in emails can sometimes be perceived as harsh or abrupt by team members."	"That's just the way I communicate. I don't have time to sugarcoat things."	"I understand that you're busy and need to be efficient. However, a slightly softer tone can go a long way in maintaining team morale. How about we try using a template or some key phrases that convey your message while also sounding more approachable?"

By incorporating advanced techniques such as the SBI model, the Feedforward approach, and strategies for handling defensive reactions, you can enhance your feedback skills and create a more constructive and supportive feedback culture within your team.

CHAPTER 4
How to Receive Feedback Effectively

Key Practices for Receiving Feedback

Receiving feedback is as important as giving it. Effective feedback reception involves active listening, thoughtful consideration, and constructive responses. Here are the key practices to keep in mind:

1. Listen Actively:
Give your full attention to the feedback provider.
Avoid interrupting and show engagement through body language and eye contact.
Example: Nod to show understanding and wait until the feedback provider has finished speaking before responding.

2. Seek Clarification:
If any part of the feedback is unclear, ask specific questions to fully understand the observations and expectations.
Example: *"Can you provide an example of when this behavior occurred?"*

3. Summarize and Reflect:
Paraphrase what you've heard to confirm your understanding. This also helps clarify the feedback for both parties.
Example: *"So, you're saying that I need to be more proactive in team meetings. Is that correct?"*

4. Respond Appropriately:
Acknowledge the feedback received, even if you do not agree with all aspects of it.
Example: *"Thank you for your feedback. I appreciate you bringing this to my attention."*

5. Take Time to Process:
Allow yourself time to think about the feedback, especially if it is complex or emotional. This helps in responding thoughtfully rather than reactively.
Example: *"I'd like some time to think about this. Can we discuss it further tomorrow?"*

6. Develop an Action Plan:
Decide whether and how to use the feedback for improvement. Create specific, actionable steps to address the feedback.
Example: *"I will work on organizing my tasks better to meet deadlines. I'll start by using a project management tool."*

7. Follow Up:
If applicable, update the feedback giver on your progress. This demonstrates your commitment to improving and helps maintain open lines of communication.
Example: *"I've implemented your suggestion to use a project management tool, and it has already made a difference in meeting my deadlines."*

Practical Tips for Receiving Feedback

1. Stay Open-Minded:
Approach feedback with a willingness to learn and improve. Avoid becoming defensive or dismissive.
Example: Instead of thinking, *"I already know this,"* consider, *"What can I learn from this feedback?"*

2. Manage Your Emotions:
Receiving feedback, especially negative feedback, can be emotional. Take deep breaths and try to remain calm.
Example: If you feel overwhelmed, it's okay to request a short break before continuing the discussion.

3. Show Appreciation:
Thank the feedback provider for their input. This encourages a positive feedback culture.
Example: *"Thank you for your feedback. I value your insights and will work on improving."*

4. Reflect on the Feedback:
Spend time thinking about the feedback and how it applies to your work or behavior. Reflect on both strengths and areas for improvement.
Example: Write down the feedback and any immediate thoughts or feelings about it. Review it after some time for deeper reflection.

5. Separate the Feedback from the Person:
Focus on the content of the feedback rather than on the person delivering it. This helps to avoid taking feedback personally.
Example: Concentrate on the specific behaviors mentioned rather than feeling criticized as a person.

6. Ask for Examples:
Request specific examples to better understand the feedback and how to apply it.
Example: *"Can you give me an example of a situation where I could have handled things differently?"*

7. Look for Patterns:
Identify recurring themes or patterns in the feedback you receive. This can highlight areas that need more attention.
Example: If multiple people mention that you need to improve your communication skills, it's likely an area worth focusing on.

Examples of Effective Feedback Reception

1. Receiving Positive Feedback:
Scenario: A team member receives praise for their project management skills.
Response: *"Thank you! I'm glad my approach is working well. If you have any suggestions for further improvement, I'd love to hear them."*

2. Receiving Constructive Feedback:
Scenario: A team member is told they need to improve their time management.
Response: *"I understand that my time management needs improvement. I appreciate your feedback and will work on prioritizing my tasks better."*

3. Receiving Challenging Feedback:
Scenario: A team member is criticized for their communication style.
Response: *"I didn't realize my communication style was an issue. Can you give me some specific examples and suggestions for improvement?"*

Developing an Action Plan

After receiving feedback, it's important to develop an action plan to address the areas of improvement:

1. Identify Key Areas for Improvement:
Pinpoint the specific behaviors or skills that need enhancement based on the feedback.

2. Set SMART Goals:
Create Specific, Measurable, Achievable, Relevant, and Time-bound goals to address the feedback.
Example: *"I will improve my time management by using a daily planner and setting reminders for deadlines."*

3. Seek Support and Resources:
Identify resources, such as training programs, mentors, or tools, that can help you improve.
Example: *"I will attend a time management workshop next month."*

4. Monitor Progress:
Regularly review your progress towards your goals and adjust your action plan as needed.
Example: *"I will review my planner weekly to ensure I'm staying on track with my deadlines."*

5. Request Feedback on Progress:
Ask for follow-up feedback to gauge your improvement and make further adjustments.
Example: *"Can we have a follow-up meeting next month to discuss my progress on time management?"*

> *By practicing these key principles and tips, you can receive feedback effectively, turning it into a powerful tool for personal and professional growth. This approach not only enhances your individual performance but also contributes to building a resilient and high-performing team.*

CHAPTER 5
Evaluating Feedback Effectiveness

EVALUATING FEEDBACK EFFECTIVENESS

Effective feedback is crucial for fostering growth and improvement within a team. However, to ensure that feedback practices are genuinely beneficial, it's essential to evaluate their effectiveness continuously. This chapter provides detailed guidance on how to measure the impact of feedback, the tools needed for evaluation, and a continuous improvement plan to enhance feedback practices.

Feedback Metrics

Feedback metrics are essential for quantifying the effectiveness of feedback practices within a team. By tracking these metrics, managers can gain insights into how often feedback is given, the quality of the feedback, and its impact on performance and engagement. Here are key metrics to consider:

1. Feedback Frequency

Definition: The regularity with which feedback is given and received within the team.

Importance: Regular feedback ensures continuous improvement and timely correction of issues.

Measurement: Track the number of feedback sessions held per month and compare it to established goals.

2. Impact on Performance

Definition: The extent to which feedback contributes to improvements in individual and team performance.

Importance: Feedback should lead to measurable improvements in skills, productivity, and overall performance.

Measurement: Use performance reviews and key performance indicators (KPIs) to assess changes in performance pre- and post-feedback.

3. Employee Engagement

Definition: The level of enthusiasm and commitment employees feel towards their work and organization.

Importance: Effective feedback can enhance employee engagement by making them feel valued and supported.

Measurement: Conduct regular engagement surveys and compare scores over time to identify trends.

4. Feedback Quality

Definition: The clarity, constructiveness, and usefulness of the feedback provided.

Importance: High-quality feedback is specific, actionable, and supportive, leading to better outcomes.

Measurement: Use feedback surveys to gather perceptions of feedback quality from both givers and receivers.

5. Behavioral Changes

Definition: Observable changes in behavior that result from the feedback given.

Importance: Behavioral changes indicate that feedback is being effectively internalized and acted upon.

Measurement: Monitor specific behaviors over time and assess changes through observations and self-reports.

Evaluation Tools

To thoroughly evaluate feedback practices, having the right tools at your disposal is crucial. Let us look how various tools, including surveys and self-assessment checklists, may help you gather valuable data on feedback frequency, quality, and impact. These tools are designed to facilitate self-reflection, peer assessment, and the monitoring of behavioral changes, ensuring a well-rounded evaluation process.

1. Feedback Frequency Survey

Purpose: To gauge how often feedback is given and received within the team.

Sample Questions:

- How often do you receive/provide feedback from your manager?
- How often do you receive/provide feedback to your colleagues?

- Do you feel the frequency of feedback sessions is sufficient?

2. Feedback Quality Survey

Purpose: To assess the quality and impact of feedback.

Sample Questions:

- How clear and specific was the feedback you received?
- Was the feedback actionable and useful for your improvement?
- Did the feedback help you understand your strengths and areas for development?

3. Self-Assessment Checklist

Purpose: To help individuals reflect on their feedback practices.

Sample Items:

- I provide feedback regularly to my team members.
- I ensure my feedback is specific and based on observable behaviors.
- I seek feedback from my peers and superiors to improve my performance.
- I act on the feedback I receive to enhance my skills and productivity.

4. Behavioral Change Observation Form

Purpose: To document changes in behavior following feedback.

Sample Items:

- Behavior observed before feedback (describe).
- Specific feedback given (details).
- Behavior observed after feedback (describe).
- Additional comments on observed changes.

Continuous Improvement Plan

A continuous improvement plan is vital for maintaining and enhancing feedback practices over time. Below you find a step-by-step plan to ensure ongoing evaluation and refinement of feedback strategies. By establishing baseline metrics, setting clear goals, providing training, and regularly monitoring progress, managers can foster a culture of continuous development and excellence. This approach not only addresses current feedback challenges but also anticipates future needs, ensuring sustained improvement.

1. Establish Baseline Metrics

Action: Conduct initial surveys and assessments to gather baseline data on feedback frequency, quality, and impact.

Outcome: Establish a reference point to measure future improvements against.

2. Set Clear Goals

Action: Define specific, measurable goals for feedback practices, such as increasing feedback frequency or improving feedback quality scores.

Outcome: Clear targets to aim for and track progress.

3. Provide Training and Resources

Action: Offer training sessions and resources to enhance feedback skills, including workshops, online courses, and coaching.

Outcome: Improved capability and confidence in giving and receiving feedback.

4. Implement Regular Check-Ins

Action: Schedule regular check-ins to discuss feedback experiences, challenges, and successes.

Outcome: Continuous support and reinforcement of good feedback practices.

5. Monitor Progress

Action: Use the evaluation tools (surveys, checklists, observation forms) to regularly monitor progress towards goals.

Outcome: Ongoing data collection to inform adjustments and improvements.

6. Adjust Strategies as Needed

Action: Based on the evaluation data, adjust feedback strategies to address identified weaknesses or enhance strengths.

Outcome: Continuous refinement of feedback practices to ensure they remain effective and relevant.

7. Celebrate Successes

Action: Recognize and celebrate improvements and milestones achieved through effective feedback practices.

Outcome: Increased motivation and reinforcement of positive behaviors.

> *By systematically evaluating feedback practices using these metrics, tools, and a continuous improvement plan, managers can ensure that feedback remains a powerful tool for enhancing performance, engagement, and team dynamics. This approach not only helps in identifying areas for improvement but also in sustaining a culture of continuous development and excellence.*

CHAPTER 6
Feedback Across Cultures

FEEDBACK ACROSS CULTURES

In today's globalized work environment, teams often comprise members from diverse cultural backgrounds. This diversity can enrich the workplace with a variety of perspectives and approaches. However, it also presents challenges, particularly in how feedback is given and received. Understanding and addressing cultural differences in feedback practices is crucial for fostering effective communication and collaboration within multicultural teams. This chapter will explore common cultural barriers to feedback, provide case studies of feedback in multicultural teams, and recommend resources and training programs to enhance cultural sensitivity.

Cultural Barriers and Solutions

Cultural differences can significantly impact the way feedback is perceived and delivered. Recognizing and addressing these barriers is essential for ensuring that feedback is constructive and well-received across diverse teams. This subchapter will discuss common cultural barriers to feedback and provide practical solutions for overcoming them.

Direct vs. Indirect Communication Styles

Barrier: In some cultures, direct communication is valued and seen as clear and honest, while in others, indirect communication is preferred to avoid confrontation and maintain harmony.

Solution: Adapt your communication style to match the recipient's preference. Use indirect language for cultures that value subtlety, and be clear and explicit for those that value directness. For example, instead of saying *"Your report was incorrect,"* try *"It might be helpful to review the report again for any possible errors."*

High-Context vs. Low-Context Cultures

Barrier: High-context cultures rely on implicit communication and shared understanding, whereas low-context cultures value explicit and clear communication.

Solution: Provide detailed explanations and context for feedback when working with high-context cultures. Ensure that all relevant information is conveyed to avoid misunderstandings.

Power Distance

Barrier: In high power distance cultures, there is a greater acceptance of hierarchical order and unequal power distribution, which can make subordinates less likely to provide feedback to superiors.

Solution: Create a safe and respectful environment where team members feel comfortable providing feedback regardless of their position. Encourage open dialogue and make it clear that feedback is valued from all levels of the organization.

Face-Saving

Barrier: In cultures that place a high value on maintaining face and avoiding embarrassment, direct criticism can be damaging to relationships and self-esteem.

Solution: Frame feedback in a way that preserves dignity. Use positive reinforcement and constructive suggestions. For instance, highlight what was done well before suggesting areas for improvement.

Individualism vs. Collectivism

Barrier: Individualistic cultures emphasize personal achievements and autonomy, while collectivist cultures value group harmony and collective success.

Solution: Tailor feedback to align with cultural values. In collectivist cultures, emphasize team achievements and collaborative efforts, while in individualistic cultures, highlight personal accomplishments and individual contributions.

Case Studies

Examining real-life examples of feedback in multicultural teams can provide valuable insights into how cultural differences play out in practice. Let us look at a few case studies from our consulting practice that illustrate challenges and solutions in delivering and receiving feedback across cultures.

Case Study 1: Bridging Communication Styles

Scenario: A team with members from the United States (low-context, direct communication) and Japan (high-context, indirect communication) faced misunderstandings during project feedback sessions.

Solution: The team implemented a structured feedback process using written summaries and visual aids to ensure clarity. They also held cultural awareness workshops to help members understand each other's communication preferences.

Case Study 2: Addressing Power Distance

Scenario: In a team with a mix of European (low power distance) and Middle Eastern (high power distance) members, junior employees from the Middle East were hesitant to give feedback to their European managers.

Solution: The organization introduced anonymous feedback tools and regular, informal check-ins to create a more open and inclusive feedback culture. Managers also received training on how to encourage feedback from all team members.

Case Study 3: Maintaining Face

Scenario: A multinational company with a significant presence in China (high face-saving culture) struggled with delivering constructive criticism without causing offense.

Solution: The company adopted a feedback sandwich approach, where positive feedback is given before and after constructive criticism. They also trained managers in culturally sensitive communication techniques.

Cultural Sensitivity Training

To effectively navigate cultural differences in feedback, managers and teams need to develop cultural sensitivity. This subchapter will recommend resources and training programs that can enhance cultural awareness and improve feedback practices in multicultural environments.

Training Programs

Cross-Cultural Communication Workshops: These workshops provide insights into different communication styles and cultural norms, helping participants understand and adapt to diverse feedback preferences.

Diversity and Inclusion Training: Programs that focus on fostering an inclusive workplace culture where all voices are heard and respected, regardless of cultural background.

Both types of workshops are offered by Team World and can be tailored to your situation and needs.

Online Courses and Webinars

Coursera and Udemy: Both platforms offer courses on intercultural communication, global leadership, and managing multicultural teams.

Korn Ferry: Offers specific courses on cultural agility and navigating cultural differences in the workplace.

Books and Articles

"The Culture Map" by Erin Meyer: This book provides a framework for understanding cultural differences in communication, including feedback.

Harvard Business Review Articles: Numerous pieces on managing multicultural teams and giving feedback across cultures. Here are two inspiring articles to get you started:

Vasyl Taras, Dan Baack, Dan Caprar, Alfredo Jiménez, and Fabian Froese (2021), Research: How Cultural Differences Can Impact Global Teams, Link

Andy Molinsky and Melissa Hahn (2024), Building Cross-Cultural Relationships in a Global Workplace, Link

Internal Resources

Employee Resource Groups (ERGs): ERGs are voluntary, employee-led groups whose aim is to foster a diverse, inclusive workplace aligned with the organizations they serve. Encourage the formation of ERGs focused on cultural awareness and inclusion, providing a platform for employees to share experiences and best practices.

Mentorship Programs: Pair employees with mentors from different cultural backgrounds to foster mutual learning and understanding.

By understanding and addressing cultural barriers, leveraging case studies, and investing in cultural sensitivity training, managers can enhance their ability to give and receive feedback effectively within multicultural teams. This approach not only improves communication but also fosters a more inclusive and collaborative work environment.

CHAPTER 7
Strengthen Your Team's Feedback Muscle with Feedback Cards and Exercises

STRENGTHEN YOUR TEAM'S FEEDBACK MUSCLE WITH FEEDBACK CARDS AND EXERCISES

By now, you will have understood that feedback is like a muscle—something that can be actively trained, but also something that needs to be used regularly to sustain its power. Feedback cards are a practical and interactive tool designed to help teams practice the art of giving and receiving feedback. Each card presents a specific scenario, offering a structured way to simulate real-life feedback situations. The scenarios cover a wide range of common workplace behaviors, both positive and negative, and provide a guided approach to delivering and responding to feedback.

You can easily prepare your own feedback cards to fit with your specific situation and context. To make these exercises even more accessible and engaging, a set of preprinted feedback cards is available from Team World at https://team-world.de/. These cards can be purchased directly from the Team World website, ensuring that your team has a ready-to-use resource for improving feedback skills. By utilizing these preprinted cards, teams can seamlessly integrate feedback practice into their regular meetings and training sessions, fostering a culture of open communication and continuous improvement.

Purpose of the Feedback Cards

The feedback cards serve multiple purposes:

Practice: They provide a safe environment to practice giving and receiving feedback.
Reflection: They encourage reflection on personal and team behaviors.
Skill Development: They help develop essential communication and feedback skills.
Team Building: They foster a culture of open communication and continuous improvement within teams.

How to Use the Feedback Cards

Below are ten exercises and uses for the feedback cards to help you and your team to effectively practice and master feedback skills.

1. Role-Play Scenarios

Objective: To practice giving and receiving feedback in a simulated environment.
Instructions:

- Divide the team into pairs or small groups.
- Each group receives a card with a specific scenario.
- One person plays the role of the feedback giver, and the other(s) play the feedback receiver(s).

- Act out the scenario, focusing on providing constructive feedback and responding appropriately.
- After each role-play, discuss what went well and what could be improved.

Example:

- Scenario: "Accountability for Mistakes"
- Feedback Giver: "I noticed you admitted to making an error in the report and took steps to correct it. This builds trust within the team."
- Feedback Receiver: "Thank you for the feedback. I'll continue to own up to my mistakes and work on improving."

2. Feedback Circle
Objective: To create a continuous flow of feedback among team members.
Instructions:

- Form a circle with the team members.
- Each participant draws a card and gives feedback based on the scenario to the person on their right.
- This continues around the circle until everyone has given and received feedback.
- After completing the circle, hold a group discussion to share insights and reflections.

Example:

- Scenario: "Enhancing Team Morale"
- Feedback Giver: "I've seen how you organize team events, which really boosts our morale. It's great for team spirit."
- Feedback Receiver: "Thank you! I'll keep looking for ways to keep the team motivated."

3. Real-Life Application
Objective: To apply feedback scenarios to actual workplace situations.
Instructions:

- Ask participants to think of a real-life situation where they observed a similar behavior as described on the card they drew.
- Use the card as a guide to provide feedback based on that real-life situation.
- Share the feedback with the group and discuss the application to real-life contexts.

Example:

- Scenario: "Professionalism in Client Interactions"
- Real-Life Situation: A team member's exemplary communication with a difficult client.
- Feedback: "Your professionalism in handling the client's complaints was outstanding. It

maintained our relationship and demonstrated our commitment to service."

4. Group Discussion and Analysis

Objective: To deepen understanding and share best practices for giving and receiving feedback.

Instructions:

- Select a few cards and read the scenarios aloud to the entire group.
- Have an open discussion about the importance of each scenario and how similar situations have been handled in the past.
- Discuss the best ways to give and receive feedback in those contexts and share experiences and tips.

Example:

- Scenario: "Resisting Feedback"
- Discussion: Why do people resist feedback, and how can we create an environment where feedback is welcomed?

5. Feedback Practice Sessions

Objective: To provide dedicated practice opportunities for feedback skills.

Instructions:

- Hold dedicated feedback practice sessions where team members pair up and randomly draw cards to role-play feedback scenarios.
- After each session, discuss as a group what went well, what was challenging, and how they can improve.
- Rotate pairs and repeat the exercise to provide varied practice experiences.

Example:

- Scenario: "Low Engagement in Team Projects"
- Feedback Giver: "I've noticed you're often quiet during team meetings. Your input is valuable, and we'd love to hear more from you."
- Feedback Receiver: "I'll make an effort to contribute more. Thank you for encouraging me."

6. Scenario-Based Training

Objective: To integrate feedback cards into broader training programs.

Instructions:

- Incorporate the cards into training sessions focused on feedback, communication, or performance management.
- Use the scenarios as case studies for participants to analyze and discuss.

- Develop role-play or discussion activities based on the scenarios to reinforce learning objectives.

Example:

- Scenario: "Effective Meeting Facilitation"
- Training Activity: Discuss the elements of effective meeting facilitation and role-play a meeting with feedback provided based on the scenario.

7. Feedback Simulation Game

Objective: To make feedback practice engaging and competitive.

Instructions:

- Turn the exercise into a game where points are awarded for effective feedback.
- Criteria can include clarity, constructiveness, and empathy.
- Each scenario from the cards can be a different round, and team members can vote or a facilitator can judge the feedback provided.

Example:

- Scenario: "Innovation in Project Management"
- Feedback: Points awarded for specific, actionable, and positively framed feedback.

8. Reflective Writing Exercise

Objective: To encourage thoughtful reflection on feedback scenarios.

Instructions:

- Have team members select a card and write a reflective piece on how they would give feedback in the scenario.
- They can also write about a time they either received or gave feedback in a similar situation.
- Share reflections with the group to discuss different perspectives and approaches.

Example:

- Scenario: "Strong Analytical Skills"
- Reflective Writing: "I would praise the individual's problem-solving abilities and suggest they share their analytical methods with the team to foster a culture of continuous learning."

9. Improvisation Challenge

Objective: To enhance quick thinking and adaptability in giving feedback.

Instructions:

- Create an improvisation challenge where participants draw a card and must spontaneously give feedback based on the scenario.
- This helps improve quick thinking and adaptability in giving feedback.
- After the challenge, discuss what was easy or difficult about the improvisation.

Example:

- Scenario: "Positive Attitude in Stressful Situations"
- Improvised Feedback: "Your calm demeanor during last week's crisis helped the team stay focused and find a solution quickly."

10. Feedback Pairs with Observer

Objective: To gain insights from a third-party perspective on feedback interactions.

Instructions:

- Form pairs where one person gives feedback based on a card, the other receives it, and a third person observes.

- The observer provides feedback on the interaction, focusing on the effectiveness of communication and the response.
- Rotate roles so everyone has a chance to be the feedback giver, receiver, and observer.

Example:

- Scenario: "Building Strong Client Relationships"
- Observer Feedback: "The feedback was clear and supportive. You maintained a positive tone and provided specific examples, which made it easier for the receiver to understand and accept."

By using the feedback cards in various exercises, your team can develop strong feedback skills, enhance communication, and build a resilient, high-performing team. These activities are designed to be engaging and practical, ensuring that feedback becomes an integral and positive part of your team's culture.

CHAPTER 8
Additional Exercises to Practice Feedback Giving and Receiving

ADDITIONAL EXERCISES TO PRACTICE FEEDBACK GIVING AND RECEIVING

In addition to feedback cards, there are various other exercises that can help teams practice giving and receiving feedback effectively. These exercises are designed to enhance communication skills, build trust, and create a culture of continuous improvement.

1. Role-Playing

Role plays are an effective way to simulate real-life feedback situations and practice giving and receiving feedback in a controlled environment. Such exercises help team members become more comfortable with delivering and receiving feedback, improving their communication skills and fostering a culture of openness and continuous improvement. Some simple role playing can already be orchestrated with our Feedback Cards, as introduced in the previous chapter. But you can also expand the role play approach.

Instructions: Divide the team into pairs or small groups. Provide each group with a different feedback scenario. One person in the group plays the role of the feedback giver, while the other(s) play the role of the feedback receiver(s). After the role-play, discuss what went well and what could be improved. Focus on aspects like clarity, empathy, specificity, and the recipient's response.

Here are two scenarios to illustrate this method and giving you a blueprint for developing more tailored role plays. By following these instructions and engaging in these role-playing scenarios, team members can develop a deeper understanding of effective feedback techniques and improve their ability to communicate constructively. This exercise not only enhances individual skills but also promotes a healthier and more collaborative team environment.

Scenario 1: Addressing Missed Deadlines

Background: John, a team member, has consistently missed project deadlines over the past few months. This has caused delays in the team's overall progress and frustration among team members who depend on his timely contributions.

Roles:

Feedback Giver: Project Manager

Feedback Receiver: John

Instructions for Feedback Giver:

1. Begin by acknowledging John's contributions and setting a positive tone.
2. Clearly describe the issue of missed deadlines using specific examples.

3. Explore underlying reasons for the missed deadlines by asking open-ended questions.
4. Provide constructive suggestions for improvement and offer support.
5. Encourage John to share his perspective and collaborate on finding solutions.

Dialogue Example:

Feedback Giver: *"Hi John, I'd like to talk about the recent project deadlines. I've noticed that you've missed several deadlines over the past few months, which has impacted our team's progress. Can you help me understand what's been going on?"*

Feedback Receiver: *"I know I've been struggling with the deadlines. I've had a lot on my plate, and it's been challenging to keep up with everything."*

Feedback Giver: *"I appreciate you sharing that. Let's discuss how we can manage your workload better. One idea is to prioritize tasks more effectively or perhaps delegate some responsibilities. What do you think?"*

Feedback Receiver: *"That sounds helpful. I think prioritizing tasks would make a big difference. Maybe we could set up a weekly check-in to review my workload and deadlines?"*

Reflection & Discussion Points:

Was the feedback specific and clear?

Did the feedback giver show empathy and support?

How could the feedback be improved?

Scenario 2: Improving Communication Skills

Background: Emma, a team member, often dominates team meetings, interrupting others and not allowing for collaborative discussion. This has caused frustration among other team members and stifled the team's ability to brainstorm effectively.

Roles:

Feedback Giver: Team Lead

Feedback Receiver: Emma

Instructions for Feedback Giver:

1. Start by acknowledging Emma's enthusiasm and contributions.
2. Describe the issue of dominating meetings with specific examples.
3. Explain the impact of this behavior on the team.

4. Suggest strategies for more inclusive communication, such as a 'round-robin' approach.
5. Invite Emma to share her thoughts and collaborate on improving team dynamics.

Dialogue Example:

Feedback Giver: *"Hi Emma, I'd like to talk about our team meetings. I've noticed that you often take the lead in discussions, which shows your enthusiasm. However, I've also seen that it can sometimes prevent others from sharing their ideas. Can we discuss how we might create a more balanced dialogue?"*

Feedback Receiver: *"I didn't realize I was dominating the meetings. I just get excited about the projects. What can I do to help improve the situation?"*

Feedback Giver: *"Your passion is valuable, but let's try implementing a 'round-robin' approach where everyone has a chance to speak. Also, waiting for others to finish before jumping in could make the discussions more inclusive. How does that sound?"*

Feedback Receiver: *"That makes sense. I'll be more mindful of giving others space to share their ideas and will try the round-robin approach in our next meeting."*

Discussion Points:

Was the feedback constructive and focused on specific behaviors?

Did the feedback giver provide actionable suggestions?

How did the feedback receiver respond, and what could have been done differently?

2. 360-Degree Feedback

As the name suggests, 360-Degree Feedback provides a comprehensive view of an individual's performance from multiple perspectives, including peers, subordinates, and superiors. This method helps individuals gain a well-rounded understanding of their strengths and areas for improvement, promoting personal and professional development. Here is a simple step-by-step guide to establish a 360-Degree Feedback routine in your team:

Preparation: Identify the individual who will receive the 360-degree feedback. Select a diverse group of feedback providers, including peers, subordinates, and superiors. Aim for a balanced representation to get a full spectrum of perspectives, while keeping the load manageable. Involve the colleague who will receive the feedback also in suggesting and selecting reviewers.

/// ADDITIONAL EXERCISES TO PRACTICE FEEDBACK GIVING AND RECEIVING

Decide for or Design Feedback Form: Choose or develop a feedback form that includes questions and rating scales covering key performance areas such as teamwork, communication, leadership, technical skills, and other relevant competencies. It makes sense to include both quantitative (rating scales) and qualitative (open-ended questions) components to gather detailed feedback. Here is a simple template from our consulting practice:

360 degree feedback form for employee evaluation

Time spent	Every Day	A few times a week	A few times a month	Every few months	n.a. / never
Your interaction with employee		X			

	Strongly Agree	Agree	Disagree	Strongly Disagree	n.a.
Work Quality					
Sets high standards for quality of work output	X				
Ensures work is free from errors before submitting		X			
Assists peers to improve quality		X			
Communication & Interaction					
Communicates well orally and in written form		X			
Actively listens to others			X		
Shares information freely with others		X			
Team Work					
Contributes positively to the team	X				
Assists others to maximize output		X			
Can be counted on to complete tasks correctly	X				

Share Form: Distribute the feedback forms to the selected feedback providers. Decide whether you want to have anonymous feedback (resulting in more honest feedback) or whether the feedback givers should be disclosed later to the receiver. Share this information together with the forms.

Collect and Analyze Feedback: Collect the completed forms and compile the feedback into a comprehensive report, highlighting common themes, strengths, and areas for improvement.

Conduct Feedback Session: Schedule a one-on-one feedback session with the individual. Present the feedback report, discussing key findings and specific examples. Encourage the individual to reflect on the feedback and ask questions for clarification.

Develop an Action Plan: Work with the individual to develop a personalized action plan based on the feedback. Set specific, measurable, achievable, relevant, and time-bound (SMART) goals for improvement. Identify resources and support needed to achieve these goals, such as training, mentoring, or additional feedback sessions.

Follow-Up: Schedule regular follow-up meetings (or make room in your regular one-on-ones) to review progress and adjust the action plan as needed. Continue to provide ongoing support and encouragement.

3. Feedback Journals

Feedback journals are a powerful tool for personal and professional growth. They provide a structured way for individuals to record and reflect on the feedback they encounter in their daily work life. By keeping a feedback journal, team members can track their development over time, identify patterns in the feedback they receive, and take proactive steps to improve their performance and interactions.

This method emphasizes the importance of continuous learning and self-awareness. It encourages individuals to take ownership of their growth and actively seek out feedback, rather than passively receiving it. By documenting both the feedback given to others and the feedback received, team members can develop a holistic view of their communication and leadership skills.

Feedback journals also foster a culture of accountability and transparency. When team members regularly review and reflect on their feedback, they become more mindful of their actions and their impact on others. This heightened awareness can lead to more constructive and meaningful interactions, ultimately enhancing team dynamics and performance.

Instructions: Ask team members to keep a feedback journal where they record feedback they give and receive. Include reflections on how the feedback was delivered, how it was received, and what actions were taken as a result. Make sure to regularly review the journal either individually or as a team to share insights and discuss improvements.

> Team World offers a printed feedback journal. In addition to a short summary of key principles for giving and receiving feedback it offers 100 pages to captures given as well as received feedback. Check out www.team-world.de for more details.

4. Peer Review Sessions

Peer review sessions are a great way to provide structured opportunities for team members to give and receive constructive feedback on specific tasks or projects. This method helps individuals improve their work by leveraging the diverse perspectives and expertise of their peers.

Instructions: Organize regular peer review sessions where team members present their work and receive constructive feedback from their peers. Focus on specific aspects such as content quality, presentation style, and adherence to guidelines. Ensure feedback is specific, actionable, and supportive.

/// ADDITIONAL EXERCISES TO PRACTICE FEEDBACK GIVING AND RECEIVING

Here is an example of how such a session could be organized

Peer Review Session: Review of a Draft Report

Select Participants: Identify the team members who will participate in the peer review session. Ensure a mix of roles and expertise to provide a well-rounded review.

Define Objectives: Clearly articulate the purpose of the peer review session. Whether it's for a specific project, report, presentation, or another deliverable, ensure all participants understand the goals.

Establish Guidelines: Set some overall rules to help the session stay focused. This could include Constructive Feedback (emphasize the importance of providing feedback that is specific, actionable, and supportive), Respect and Confidentiality: (ensure that all feedback is given respectfully and that the contents of the peer review remain confidential), Time Management (allocate specific times for each review to ensure the session stays on schedule).

Execution

Present the Work: Each participant presents their work to the group. This could be a project update, draft report, presentation, or any other relevant deliverable. Provide context and background information to help reviewers understand the scope and objectives of the work being reviewed.

Structured Feedback: Each reviewer takes turns providing their feedback. Ensure that feedback is balanced, focusing on both strengths and areas for improvement. Encourage reviewers to be specific and use examples to illustrate their points. One effective model is the "What Went Well, Even Better If" (WWW-EBI) approach:

What Went Well (WWW): Highlight the strengths and positive aspects of the work.

Even Better If (EBI): Provide specific suggestions for improvement.

Recipient Reflection: After receiving feedback, the presenter has an opportunity to ask clarifying questions and reflect on the feedback received. This reflection can help the presenter understand the feedback more deeply and consider how to apply it.

Follow-Up: At the end of or after the peer review session, the presenter develops an action plan based on the feedback received. This plan should include specific steps for improvement, resources needed, and timelines. You can then schedule follow-up sessions to review the progress made on

> the action plan and the targeted improvements of the product. This can help ensure that feedback is implemented effectively and provides ongoing support and accountability.
>
> **Continuous Improvement:** Encourage team members to continuously seek and provide peer feedback as part of their regular workflow. This fosters a culture of ongoing improvement and collaboration.

5. Real-Time Feedback Practice

As you may not always have the opportunity and resources to conduct tailored peer review sessions, you should also seek to practice giving and receiving feedback in real-time during team activities.

Instructions: During team meetings or collaborative projects, encourage team members to provide real-time feedback. Focus on immediate behaviors and actions, ensuring feedback is constructive and aimed at improving performance. Use a structured approach like the SBI model (Situation-Behavior-Impact) to deliver feedback.

Example: During a meeting, one team member might say, "I noticed you took the lead on the discussion (Situation). You did a great job keeping us on track (Behavior). This really helped us cover all the agenda items efficiently (Impact)."

6. Kudos Cards / Sticky Notes

You can also encourage ongoing, informal feedback in a non-intrusive way, for example through the sharing of "Kudos" cards or sticky notes.

Instructions: Provide team members with printed "Kudos" cards or sticky notes and designate a specific area in the office (like a feedback board) where they can post feedback for their colleagues. Use the cards yourself to give feedback to team members and encourage others to also give quick, specific feedback or appreciation throughout the day. Regularly review the feedback posted and discuss it in team meetings to reinforce positive behaviors and address any issues.

Team World offers some free Kudos Card templates as well as a set of printed Kudo Cards for ordering:

Check out www.team-world.de for more details.

7. Feedback Round Robin

A round robin feedback exercise is a simple way to create multiple opportunities for giving and receiving feedback in a short period. It can be integrated easily into existing team formats such as your weekly or monthly team meetings, and can even be used as an icebreaker before or between other meeting formats.

Instructions: Arrange team members in a circle or line. Each person gives feedback to the person next to them, focusing on one specific area (e.g., communication, teamwork). After receiving feedback, the person moves to the next participant and gives feedback, continuing the process until everyone has interacted.

8. Dedicated Feedback & Reflection Workshops

In addition to these regular team routines and activities you can also dedicate a full workshop to build feedback skills through guided practice and discussion.

Instructions: Organize workshops focused on feedback skills, including exercises, discussions, and role-plays. Cover topics such as the importance of feedback, effective feedback techniques, and common challenges. Facilitate practice sessions where participants give and receive feedback, followed by group discussions to share experiences and tips. Here is a sample agenda for a half-day feedback workshop:

Example Workshop Agenda (:

1. Brainstorming about how to best give and receive feedback. (30min)
2. Agreement on common feedback principles. (30min)
3. Role-playing exercises in small groups. (60min)
4. Group reflection and discussion on observed challenges and solutions. (30min)
5. Practice sessions with real-time feedback and group debrief. (30min)

By incorporating these exercises into your team's routine, you can help them develop stronger feedback skills, enhance communication, and build a culture of continuous improvement. These activities provide diverse opportunities for practicing feedback, ensuring that team members become more comfortable and effective in both giving and receiving it.

CONCLUSION

Mastering Feedback for Team Development and Continuous Improvement

As we conclude this playbook on mastering feedback, it's important to reflect on the journey we've taken together and the key insights we've uncovered. This book has equipped you with the knowledge and tools necessary to foster a robust feedback culture within your team, transforming feedback from a mere formality into a powerful catalyst for growth, development, and sustained success. Let's look at a few key takeaways, before looking at a path to implement these learnings in your team and in your leadership routines.

The Importance of Feedback: Feedback is a critical element in today's fast-paced, ever-evolving work environment. It serves as a catalyst for growth, learning, and continuous improvement, helping individuals and teams navigate complexities and adapt to new challenges.

Understanding Feedback: Feedback is not just about correction; it is a nuanced communication tool that requires clarity, precision, and empathy. Effective feedback focuses on specific behaviors, provides actionable advice, and encourages positive change.

Giving Feedback: The principles of giving feedback emphasize being descriptive, specific, and supportive. Techniques like the WWW model (What I Observed, Why It Matters, What I Wish) and advanced methods such as the SBI (Situation-Behavior-Impact) model ensure feedback is clear and constructive.

Receiving Feedback: Receiving feedback effectively involves active listening, seeking clarification, and responding appropriately. It's crucial to approach feedback with an open mind, manage emotions, and develop an action plan for improvement.

Feedback Practices and Exercises: Practical exercises and feedback cards provide structured scenarios for practicing feedback skills. These tools help teams simulate real-life situations and develop a consistent and effective feedback routine.

Evaluating Feedback Effectiveness: Regularly evaluating feedback practices using metrics such as frequency, quality, impact on performance, and behavioral changes ensures continuous improvement. Utilizing surveys, self-assessment checklists, and observation forms helps track progress and identify areas for enhancement.

Feedback Across Cultures: Understanding cultural differences in feedback practices is crucial in a globalized work environment. Addressing cultural barriers, examining case studies, and engaging in cultural sensitivity training helps foster a more inclusive and effective feedback culture.

A Way Forward for Leaders and Managers

As a leader, your role in cultivating a feedback-rich environment is pivotal. Your actions and attitudes set the tone for the entire team, making it essential for you to model the behaviors you wish to see in others. By actively engaging in feedback processes, you demonstrate its importance and create a culture where open communication is valued and encouraged. Your willingness to seek feedback on your own performance shows humility and a commitment to personal growth, which inspires your team members to do the same.

Moreover, as a leader, you have the responsibility to ensure that feedback is not only given frequently but also constructively. This means providing training and resources to help your team develop their feedback skills, and establishing clear guidelines and practices that make feedback a regular part of daily operations. Your proactive approach to addressing feedback-related challenges and your dedication to continuous improvement will help build trust and foster a supportive environment where everyone feels comfortable sharing their insights and suggestions.

By prioritizing feedback, you help your team navigate challenges, enhance their skills, and achieve higher levels of performance. Your role is not just to manage but to coach and develop your team, leveraging feedback as a tool for collective growth and success. In this way, you not only drive individual and team development but also contribute to the overall health and effectiveness of your organization.

So let us look at seven measures that help you integrate feedback in your own leadership behavior and routines.

1. Lead by Example: Demonstrate your commitment to a feedback culture by actively seeking and providing feedback. Model the behaviors you wish to see in your team.

2. Encourage Open Communication: Foster an environment where team members feel safe and valued when giving and receiving feedback. Encourage open dialogue and make it clear that feedback is a tool for growth, not criticism.

3. Implement Regular Feedback Sessions: Schedule regular feedback sessions to ensure continuous improvement and timely resolution of issues. Make feedback an integral part of team meetings and performance reviews.

4. Utilize Feedback Tools and Resources: Leverage the feedback cards, evaluation tools, and exercises provided in this playbook. These resources are designed to help you practice and refine your feedback skills consistently.

5. Invest in Training and Development: Provide ongoing training and development opportunities for your team to enhance their feedback skills. Consider cultural sensitivity training to improve communication in multicultural teams.

6. Monitor and Adjust: Regularly evaluate the effectiveness of your feedback practices. Use the metrics and tools outlined in this playbook to monitor progress and make necessary adjustments to improve the feedback process.

7. Celebrate Successes: Recognize and celebrate improvements and milestones achieved through effective feedback practices. This reinforces positive behavior and motivates the team to continue striving for excellence.

By embedding these practices into your leadership approach, you can create a support the development of a thriving feedback culture that drives continuous improvement, fosters trust, and enhances overall team performance.

Remember, feedback is not just a tool; it's a journey of mutual growth and learning. Lead your team with empathy, clarity, and a commitment to excellence, and you will unlock their full potential, ensuring sustained success in an ever-changing world.

Impressum – Legal Disclosure

Veröffentlicht durch / Published by:

Dr Nils Koenig
Wilhelmsaue 12a, 10715 Berlin
nils@team-world.de
www.team-world.de
© 2024

Verfügbar als / Available as: ebook & Paperback.

Feel free to contact us with any questions about this book, related products (e.g., Feedback Cards), or for a personalized consulting and coaching offer for your team.

Kontaktieren Sie uns gern bei Fragen rund um dieses Buch, zu damit verbundenen Produkten (z.B. Feedback Cards) oder für ein individuelles Beratungs- und Coachingangebot für Ihr Team.

www.ingramcontent.com/pod-product-compliance
Lightning Source LLC
Chambersburg PA
CBHW071214240526
45470CB00018B/1863